**Alistair**

## Captain

*with illustrations by Rebecca Glover*

# B L O O M S B U R Y

LONDON • NEW DELHI • NEW YORK • SYDNEY

**Bloomsbury Methuen Drama**

An imprint of Bloomsbury Publishing Plc

50 Bedford Square
London
WC1B 3DP
UK

1385 Broadway
New York
NY 10018
USA

**www.bloomsbury.com**

**Bloomsbury is a registered trade mark of Bloomsbury Publishing Plc**

First published 2014

**British Library Cataloguing-in-Publication Data**
A catalogue record for this book is available from the British Library

ISBN: PB: 978-1-4725-8822-7
ePub: 978-1-4725-8824-1
ePDF: 978-1-4725-8823-4

**Library of Congress Cataloging-in-Publication Data**
A catalog record for this book is available from the Library of Congress.

Typeset by Country Setting, Kingsdown, Kent CT14 8ES

presents

# Captain Amazing

by Alistair McDowall

*Captain Amazing*
was one of the winners of
Live Theatre and The Empty Space's
*FUSES: New Writing Festival*
bursaries in 2012

The play was first performed at Live Theatre
from Tuesday 9 to Saturday 13 April 2013

# Tour Dates 2014

**Traverse Theatre**
Thursday 3 to Saturday 5 April
www.traverse.co.uk
(0131) 228 1404

**Burton Taylor Studio, Oxford**
Tuesday 8 & Wednesday 9 April
www.oxfordplayhouse.com
(01865) 305 305

**Hull Truck Theatre**
Thursday 10 & Friday 11 April
www.hulltruck.co.uk
(01482) 323 638

**HighTide Festival**
Sunday 13 April
www.hightide.org.uk
(01603) 598 606

**Soho Theatre**
Wednesday 16 April to Sunday 4 May
www.sohotheatre.com
(020) 7478 0100

**Live Theatre**
Wednesday 7 to Saturday 17 May
www.live.org.uk
(0191) 232 1232

# Captain Amazing

*A funny and poignant one-man show telling the story
of a father, turned reluctant superhero, struggling
to balance his family responsibilities
with his superhero duties.*

## Creative & Production Team

| | |
|---|---|
| Writer | **Alistair McDowall** |
| Director | **Clive Judd** |
| Performer | **Mark Weinman** |
| Illustrator | **Rebecca Glover** |
| Lighting Designer | **Drummond Orr** |
| Sound Designer | **Martin Hodgson** |
| AV Designer | **Paul Aziz** |
| Production Manager | **Drummond Orr** |
| Stage Manager | **Paul Aziz** |
| Producer | **Dani Rae** |

# About the Creative Team

**Alistair McDowall**  *Writer*

Alistair is a playwright from the North East of England.

His other plays include: *Pomona* (Royal Welsh College of Music & Drama/The Gate), *Talk Show* (Royal Court) and *Brilliant Adventures* (Royal Exchange/Live Theatre). In 2011 *Brilliant Adventures* was awarded a Bruntwood Prize for Playwriting. Alistair has been on attachment with the Royal Court, Paines Plough and the National Theatre Studio.

**Clive Judd**  |  *Director*

Clive trained at the Watermill Theatre on the Regional Theatre Young Director Scheme in 2011/12. He graduated from the University of Manchester in 2008.

Credits as director include: *Romeo + Juliet* (Watermill Theatre), *Why I Don't Like The Sea* (Arcola Theatre/Lost Theatre), *Plain Jane* (Cheap Seats/Royal Exchange Theatre), *White Blood Cells* (Cheap Seats/Blacks Members Club/Temple Works), *5:30* (Cheap Seats/Library Theatre/24/7 Theatre Festival) and *Herons* (Falling Leaves/Library Theatre/NSDF09).

Credits as associate director include: *Radio Times* (Watermill Theatre/UK tour).

**Mark Weinman**  |  *Performer*

Mark studied Drama at the University of Manchester.

His stage credits include: *Prime Time* (Royal Court), *Serjeant Musgrave's Dance* (Royal Court, rehearsed reading), *Prophesy* (Blackall Studios), *Barrow Hill* (Finborough), *The Hairy Ape* (Southwark Playhouse), *Some Scary Stories* (Royal Exchange Theatre), *Step 9 (of 12)* (nominated for Best Actor OffWestEnd), *FastBurn* (KneeHigh Theatre), *Herons* (Falling Leaves/Library Theatre/NSDF09), *Amphibians* (Bridewell Theatre), *Edmond* (Theatre Royal Haymarket), *The Emperor Jones* (National Theatre), *Still Killing Time* and *Eating Ice Cream on Gaza Beach* (Soho Theatre/NYT), *Sandy 123* (Roundhouse), *Mojo* (The Underground) and *Selling Clive* (Lost Theatre).

**Rebecca Glover**  |  *Illustrator*

Rebecca is a theatre designer, scenic artist and drama practitioner. She left university with a First Class BA Joint Honours Degree in Theatre Design & Production and Theatre Studies. She has been a resident designer for The Studio@TPS and has worked as a freelance theatre designer or scenic artist for touring companies including Proteus, Strange Face, Plested and Brown, and the award-winning artist Niki McCretton.

She has also designed for art centres, museums and theatres including the Nuffield Theatre, Natural History Museum, Watermill Theatre, The Corn Exchange Theatre and the Farnham Maltings. Rebecca recently illustrated a book to accompany *Rapunzel* (Theatre of Widdershins).

**Drummond Orr** | *Lighting Designer and Production Manager*

Drummond has over thirty years' experience as a theatre electrician and stagehand, lighting designer and production manager. In that time he has toured nationally and internationally and has worked in both touring and production theatre.

Recent lighting design and production manager credits for Live Theatre include: *Cooking with Elvis, Wet House, Tyne, The Prize, Nativities, Faith & Cold Reading, A Walk On Part, The Pitmen Painters* and *Blackbird,* as well as Youth Theatre productions *The Heights, Jonathan Likes This* and annual summer festivals. Drummond also worked on *The Girl in the Yellow Dress,* a Live Theatre, Citizens Theatre and Market Theatre, Johannesburg co-production.

Drummond has also worked with the following companies: RSC, Scottish Opera, Theatre Royal Newcastle, the Gulbenkian Studio, Opera North, Vincent Dance, Told by an Idiot, Northern Stage, Merce Cunningham Dance Company, Monster Productions and Theatre Royal, Drury Lane. He also spent five years teaching Technical Theatre Skills, Stage Management and Stagecraft at National Diploma, HND and Degree level and now tutors on Live Theatre and Gateshead College's Stage and Media Production BTEC course.

**Martin Hodgson** | *Sound Designer*

Martin was born in Darlington, County Durham, and has been a sound engineer and designer for many years.

He was Head of Sound at Northern Stage, Newcastle, where his design credits included *1984, Animal Farm, Romeo and Juliet, Grimm's Tales, More Grimm's Tales, The Princess and the Goblin* and *A Clockwork Orange.*

Sound designs for Live Theatre include: *Smack Family Robinson, Toast, A Nightingale Sang, The Lovers, Keepers of the Flame* (co-production with RSC), *Geoff Dead: Disco for Sale, Up There in Lights, Me & Cilla, Top Girls, Motherland, Blackbird, Jump!, The Pitmen Painters* (National Theatre transfers; Volkstheater, Vienna; Manhattan Theatre Club, Broadway), *Tyne* and many other productions. For Bill Kenwright Productions he designed *The Governess* and *Chin Chin* for national tours and *The Pitmen Painters* and *Three Days In May* for national tours and West End runs. Recently for JASS Productions he designed *The Perfect Murder* for a national tour.

**Paul Aziz** | *AV Design and Stage Manager*

Paul has worked in theatre from 1993 when he began as a stage technician and has since worked on many productions as a freelance stage manager as well as taking on the role of production/company manager and video designer. Paul's first production for Live Theatre was *When We Were Queens* (2002). His other Live Theatre credits include: *Top Girls, Things of Dry Hours, The Pitmen Painters, A Northern Odyssey, Inheritance, A Walk On Part, Faith & Cold Reading, Nativities, Tyne* and *Wet House.*

# About Live Theatre

From its base on Newcastle's quayside, Live Theatre produces work as varied and diverse as the audiences it engages with. To do this it:

- Creates and performs new plays of world class quality

- Finds and develops creative talent

- Unlocks the potential of young people through theatre.

Founded in 1973, the theatre was transformed in 2007 with a capital redevelopment. The result is a beautifully restored and refurbished complex of five Grade II listed buildings with state-of-the-art facilities in a unique historical setting, including a 160-seat cabaret-style theatre, a studio theatre, renovated rehearsal rooms, a series of dedicated writers' rooms as well as a thriving café, bar and pub.

Live Theatre is a national leader in developing new strategies for increasing income and assets for the charity. In 2014 the company announced LiveWorks, a £10 million capital development to purchase and develop quayside-fronted land and buildings adjacent to the Theatre, to create new commercial office space, a public park and a children and young people's writing centre.

LiveWorks will join the award-winning pub *The Broad Chare*, online course www.beaplaywright.com and The Schoolhouse (an office space for SMEs), as one of Live Theatre's creative enterprises, which increases funds through new income streams. For more information see **www.live.org.uk**

Live Theatre is grateful for the support of Arts Council England and Newcastle City Council as well as its many other friends and supporters including Best Friends:

| | |
|---|---|
| Noreen Bates | Madelaine Newton |
| Jim Beirne | Elaine Orrick |
| Michael & Pat Brown | Elaine Sandy |
| Paul Callaghan | Ian & Christine Shepherdson |
| George Caulkin | Margaret & John Shipley |
| Mauyra Cushlow | Shelagh Stephenson |
| Michael & Susan Chaplin | Sting |
| Helen Coyne | Peter Straughan |
| Robson Green | Paul & Julie Tomlinson |
| Lee Hall | Nick & Melanie Tulip |
| John Jordan | Alison Walton |
| John Josephs | Kevin Whately |
| Annette Marlowe | Lucy Winskell |

Live Theatre's *Friends* receive exclusive benefits including discounted tickets and drinks, behind-the-scenes access and invitations to special events, all from as little as £5 per month.

If you are interested in joining the *Friends of Live Theatre* please visit **www.live.org.uk/friends** for more information.

# Staff at Live Theatre

| | |
|---:|:---|
| **Chief Executive** | Jim Beirne |
| **Artistic Director** | Max Roberts |
| **Operations Director** | Wendy Barnfather |
| **Director of Enterprise & Development** | Lucy Bird |
| **Director of Education & Engagement** | Helen Moore |
| **Administrator, Directors** | Clare Overton |
| **Literary Manager** | Gez Casey |
| **Creative Producer** | Graeme Thompson |
| **Administrator, Literary Team** | Degna Stone |
| **Associate Director, Literary Team** | Steve Gilroy |
| **Production Manager** | Drummond Orr |
| **Technical Manager** | Dave Flynn |
| **Technician** | Hannah Gregory |
| **Technical Apprentice** | Craig Spence |
| **Associate Director, Education & Participation** | Paul James |
| **Drama Worker** | Rachel Glover |
| **Drama Worker** | Philip Hoffmann |
| **Administrator, Education & Participation** | Sam Bell |
| **Marketing Managers** (Job Share) | Claire Cockroft, Cait Read |
| **Marketing & Press Officer** | Emma Hall |
| **Marketing & Press Assistant** | Melanie Rashbrooke |
| **Box Office Administrator** | Amy Foley |
| **Finance Officer** (Maternity Leave) | Catherine Moody |
| **Finance Assistants** | Helen Tuffnell (Maternity Cover), Nicole Huddart |
| **House Manager** | Carole Wears |
| **Deputy House Manager** | Michael Davies |
| **Duty House Managers** | Ben Young, Mark Gerrens, Chris Foley |

### Front of House & Box Office Staff

Nina Berry, Danielle Burn, Camille Burridge, Meghan Doyle, Lewis Jobson, Charlotte Kell, Caroline Liversidge, Sarah Matthews, Emily Merritt, Hannah Murphy, Tilly Riley and Molly Wright.

# Reviews

*'A perfect union of acting, writing and directing.'*
**A Younger Theatre ★★★★★**

*'An intense performance that is moving and funny in equal measure . . . What is presented on stage is a work of pure joy.'*
**What's On Stage ★★★★★**

*'It's a phenomenal achievement to nestle so much joyous, whimsy-free wonder in such a truthful, painful story.'*
**Fest Magazine ★★★★★**

*'Captain Amazing more than lives up to its name . . . You will marvel, cry and laugh.'*
**Broadway Baby ★★★★★**

*'This may well be the best one-man show you're likely to see at the Fringe this year'*
**Telegraph ★★★★**

*'We need playwrights like McDowall. He believes in potential, champions underdogs and writes with such full-blooded, big-hearted empathy that you can't help but be won over.'*
**Scotsman ★★★★**

*'Playwright Alistair McDowall has penned a sweetly affecting script'*
**Fringe Guru ★★★★**

*'An astonishing solo performance . . .'*
**Guardian**

*'Weinman's performance is exemplary'*
**British Theatre Guide**

*'What makes this sweet tale linger, however, is its emotional weight. Like any superhero worth their salt, Captain Amazing delivers quite a punch – a wounding 'kapow' right to the guts'*
**Exeunt**

## The Amazing Origins of *Captain Amazing*!
*or, How We Done What We Did*

After I graduated from university, I spent about four years working on the fringe while working part time variously at a pub, a takeaway, and then an art gallery. The unstoppable Lucy Oliver-Harrison was my producer, and the handsome Clive Judd was my frequent director.

One day in 2009, I called Clive up to let him know I'd worked out what I wanted to do next: I was going to write an hour's worth of observational stand-up material about being a superhero and I was going to perform it myself at nightclubs while pissed. I was very into Eric Bogosian at the time (still am), and this is probably why I felt such a performance would be really exciting and edgy.

It's a testament to either how nice Clive is, or just that he was as naive as I was back then, that he also decided this was a good idea, and that we should definitely do this. Maybe he just wanted to see me get beaten up by an angry crowd. But luckily for me and all of our potential audiences, we didn't get round to it as other shows and opportunities came up.

The idea resurfaced years later, after we'd both spent a lot of time working with another friend from university, Mark Weinman, who had developed into a stunning actor.

'Why don't we get Mark to do that *Captain Amazing* idea you had?' said Clive, probably, in my memory.

'But aren't I going to perform that one day?' I blustered.

Clive went silent. (Probably.)

So instead, I ran the idea past Mark and he loved it. By now I'd developed the story: it was still a piece of stand-up comedy, but the engine that drove it along was an unspoken tragedy that had caused this man to go and humiliate himself night after night in comedy clubs either as a kind of self-flagellation, or just as a way to be heard by someone. It was now becoming, as my mum likes to call them, one of my 'miserable plays'.

But the play went on the backburner for a few years as by this point the three of us were all busy doing other things – Clive and Mark were very in demand with various theatres, and I was getting really into *Battlestar Galactica*, so we all had things going on.

What most likely kicked it into action again was a monologue of mine called *Mr Noodles* that Mark performed on Halloween 2011, which was about a shy and introverted office worker who meets a violent psychopathic talking dog who convinces him to abandon all his inhibitions and give in to his animal side. It was a comedy. But the reason it was the stepping stone to *Captain Amazing* was the form: although a lot of the text was direct address to audience, there were several long passages where Mark would play the office worker and the eponymous dog and have a series of back-and-forth exchanges. Very few actors could pull this off convincingly, but Mark's energy and attack made the stage feel as though it was populated by more than one actor, and he made the play sing with life and power (I should also mention he was aided by brilliant direction from the brilliant Ned Bennett).

By this point, I had struck up a relationship with Live Theatre in Newcastle, who were considering one or two of my other plays. Once a year they, along with The Empty Space, give funds to writers, directors or artists to come to the Theatre and develop a piece of work, and the launch of this coincided with Mark and I starting to talk about the Captain again.

At the pitch meeting, I told them that we were intending to write material and then have Mark actually go and test-drive it at real open-mic nights across Newcastle, in character and in costume. This was almost certainly the main reason we were awarded the money, and it was also something I just said on the spot, and hadn't run it past Mark even once.

Luckily for him, when I actually sat down to write the thing, the stand-up format wasn't working. I wrote a huge amount of material but it didn't feel right at all – it was too on-the-nose, it was too gimmicky and, crucially, it wasn't funny.

What I *did* like were the few small exchanges I'd written between the Captain and his daughter, whom I'd christened Emily. I loved her immediately, and I loved how the two of them were struggling through conversations about the world together, so I set aside all the material I'd written prior to this, and just started writing pages and pages of their conversations.

This is very different from how I normally write; it was a much looser, throwing-a-lot-of-things-at-the-wall process, but it felt right as I started compiling all these fractured little moments from their relationship. It became very clear that this was where the real story was, and that this was the form. And as the form shifted, so did the story: the real heart of the play was now about an emotionally crippled man forced into articulacy by the arrival of his daughter. The creation of a superhero bedtime story enables him to communicate with her in ways he finds impossible otherwise, and this new-found freedom in fantasy soon starts to seep into other areas of his life too.

Content and form suddenly came together much more clearly, and I decided the whole play had to be written like this, like those exchanges I had started writing for *Mr Noodles*: the story would be written just like a normal, multi-character play, but only performed by one actor. It was a memory play, and it was also a sort of children's play for adults, like a bedtime story where your mum or dad would do all the different voices of the characters for you. It was also a sparse, open text, and while developing it at Live Theatre with Mark, almost every alteration I made was a cut rather than an addition. I wanted the text to be something for the actor to springboard from, to provide as many opportunities as possible for interesting and intimate moments with the audience. It was an actor's play, through and through.

After the development there were a lot of other projects getting juggled, so ultimately *Captain Amazing* didn't open until April 2013, in a sort-of mini-season with another of my plays, *Brilliant Adventures* (I hope one day to write a play with 'Fantastic' in the title to complete a triptych of enthusiastic titles). Clive finally got to direct it in a wonderfully clear and crisp production, and it was supported by beautiful illustrations by Rebecca Glover, which helped Mark to paint a vivid imaginary world for the characters. As a result of him being with me throughout the development, the text was custom-fitted for him, and his performance was extraordinary. He was magical and ultimately shattering, and he elevated my text into something almost mythic in quality and tone, for which I'll forever be grateful. I also have to give a mention to the fantastic Gez Casey at Live Theatre, who was the real champion of the play, and without him I doubt we'd have gotten here.

So that's how we got to this point – I hope you enjoy/enjoyed the show, or if you're just reading this as a script, I hope you enjoy/enjoyed that too. Thank you for supporting new writing for the theatre, and thank you for allowing me the pleasure and privilege of telling you a story.

*Alistair McDowall, 2014*

# Captain Amazing

*for mark*
*for clive*
*for gez*

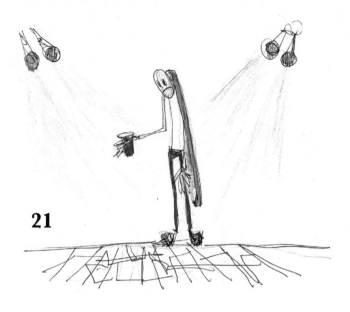

**21**

–   It's a cape.

–   It's a *cape*.

–   What?

–   It's a *cape*, what I'm wearing is a cape.

–   It's – This is a shit song. I hate this song, don't you hate
     this song?
–   I don't mind.
–   It's a shit song. You asked what I was wearing –
–   It's a cape, fine.
–   You want to know why I'm wearing it?
–   What?
–   I said, you want to know why I'm wearing a cape?

–   I'm a superhero.

–   I'm a *superhero*. Can you hear me?
     Can you *hear* me?

## 1

—  Sorry – Excuse me?
—  Mm?
—  Do you know where I can get a, uh, I need some *sealant* –
—  Sealant.
—  Yes –
—  What kind of –
—  I have a crack in my – My *sink* has a crack in it, and –
—  Your sink?
—  Yes.
—  Bathroom sink?
—  Yes.
—  Sealant won't really . . . It's a normal – ?
—  A porcelain type of a –
—  Right, bathroom sink.
—  I heard I can get some stuff to kind of, ah, *goop* into it.

—  Goop?

–    Sorry, that's stupid.


–    Uh – Well you can't really get a – How big is this crack?
–    Like – This?
–    Yeah, you can't really – We have this, but it's really just
     for painting onto tiny chips. You can't really goop it
     into big cracks.
–    We don't have to keep saying goop . . .


–    Are you renting . . . ?
–    No, I – I've just bought my first house –
–    So you won't lose your deposit then.
–    No. I just might need another sink.
–    Yeah, you probably will.


–    What?
–    Sorry.
–    You're still laughing.
–    Sorry.
–    It wasn't that funny.
–    I know, sorry.

–    Sorry.

–    What's your name?
–    I've got my –
–    Oh, yeah. Right on your – That's stupid.
–    It's alright.


–    . . .
–    . . .


–    Do you live nearby?
–    Just – Yes. Five minutes away?

–      . . .
–      . . .
–      Do you need anything else?
–      No. No, thank you.
–      Okay.
–      Alright.


–      Well. Bye.
–      Bye.

## 2

- You'll never get away with this Evil Man!
- Oh won't I? You're awfully confident for someone tied to the biggest bomb in the world, Dr Scientist Man. We'll see how sure you are once I've blown up the whole world –

Which won't be very sure, because you'll be dead.
- It's only a matter of time before Captain Amazing comes here to stop you –
- I don't think we need to worry about our friend Captain Amazing, Dr Scientist – You see, I chained him to a rocket and launched it directly into the sun. I hope he packed his sun cream – Say – Factor Two Billion?

Ahahahahahaha!
- Sorry I'm late!
- Captain Amazing!
- Gah! Curses! Not this bell end!
- Your scheme might have worked had I not been invincible against the sun, Evil Man. As it is, I just got a light tan.

–    You look great!
–    You're too late Amazing, I've already started the
        countdown. When this bomb goes off the whole
        planet will lose their heads – Literally.
–    I'm getting pretty tired of this shit, Evil Man.
–    And just to be safe, I've sealed the override switch in
        this diamond-plated granite safe!
–    Well there's one thing you hadn't counted on –
–    That'd be two things by this point –
–    There's two things you hadn't counted on – My laser
        eyes can burn through diamond and granite no
        problem.
–    You're foiled now, Evil Man!
–    Well I'll just have to launch the bomb manually!
        Ahahahahahaha!
–    After him Captain!
–    I'm going, I'm going –
–    You'll never defeat me –
–    You haven't a chance, Evil Man –


–    Ahahahaha! Once again you're too late Amazing!
–    Stop being a *dick*!
–    Argh!
–    Take this!
–    Gah –
–    And this!
–    Argg –
–    And that one was buy one get one *free* –
–    Nooooooo . . .
–    Captain Amazing! The bomb! It's launching!
–    Do you not think I can see that?
–    But I'm still tied to it!
–    Christ –
–    Captain Amaaazzziiinnnnggggg . . .
–    Hold on!

**3**

- This is nice.
- Yeah, it's alright.
- There's not many places left round here that aren't
    chains –
- Oh, it's a chain.
- Oh, right.
- Do you not like –
- No it's – I'm not being a snob or –
- Okay.
- I've just never been in –
- I've got vouchers, so –


- What?
- Nothing.


- What's funny?
- Nothing. I'm hungry.


- Can we uh – Can we get whatever we want, or do the
    vouchers – ?
- Just get what you – The vouchers aren't a big –
    I probably shouldn't have even said . . .

–   It's fine.

–   The lobster looks nice.

–   Uh – where's the – ?
–   I'm joking about the lobster.
–   If you want lobster . . .
–   No, I don't, I was just –

–   I don't want lobster.
–   Well if you do.
–   It's not even on the menu, I was just . . .


–   This is going badly isn't it?
–   No, no, it's not –
–   I'm sorry if this is shit.
–   It's not shit.
–   I don't go out with people very often, so –
–   This is fine –
–   You can leave if you want.
–   I won't,
    *judge* you.
    If that's what you want.
–   It's not.
    You're sweet.
–   Sweet?
–   Not in a – an *emasculating* –
–   Emasculating.
–   Nono, I mean –
–   What's emasculating mean?
–   Nothing. Nothing.
–   Are you alright?
–   Yes, fine. I've just got the giggles.

## 4

–   And it's had one previous owner.
–   What's the reason for selling?
–   Retirement. It's in very good condition for the price.

–   Are these the original beams?
–   I can check that for you.
–   Obviously a benefit is the open top, so you can just fly straight in, no need for a front door.
    Although, if an emergency does occur, there's a thirty-inch thick steel shield that slides across at the flick of a switch.

–   And the volcano is inactive.
–   Completely. It's not actually a volcano, it's just been designed to look as such to deter trespassers. And for the ambience.
    And, as we mentioned, there are fifteen bedrooms, twelve bathrooms, a control room, a missile silo with

four active nuclear warheads, and forty-eight holding pens.

- Holding pens?
- Basically a dungeon.
- It has a dungeon?
- I can show you if you'd –
- I don't – I'm not sure this is what I'm looking for . . .
- It's a very good price for what you're getting.
- Who was the previous owner?
- See, I'm afraid I can't *name* the seller for various reasons –
- What was his occupation?
- He was a villain.
- A villain?
- An evil genius.
- Right –
- But I assure you, once you've had a look around you'll see it can be easily refitted for your needs.
- I just – I'm really more in the market for a purpose-built superhero headquarters.
- Yes.
- I'm not really looking for a doer-upper.
- Right, yes.
- I just don't think I'll have any use for a missile silo or a dungeon.
- Mm-hm.
- I'm looking more for a Fortress of Solitude type of a property.
- I could check if Superman's interested in selling?
- No, just something *like* that. I don't – Somewhere a bit closer to home than the Arctic.
- Okay, well, why don't we shoot back to the office and look over some more suitable properties?


- Sir?
- I don't know. I'm starting to think this might be an unnecessary expense.

**5**

—     This is it then.
—     Yeah, I suppose it's – Do you want a tea?
—     Okay.


—     It's pretty sparse.
—     What?
—     You don't really have much – furniture, or –
—     I don't really have many guests.


—     Do you have another chair?
—     What?
—     Do you just have one chair, or?
—     I think I might have – There's one upstairs, or –
—     No, it's alright.
—     I can just –
—     It's fine.


—     I'll stand.


—     Bit embarrassed.
—     Don't – It's fine. It's – uncluttered.

–    This what you're reading?
–    Yeah, it's just a – a western.
–    You like westerns?
–    They're alright.
–    You read a lot?
–    I try to –
–    Do you have a lot of books, or?
–    I just use the library.
–    So it's just this one book.
–    I read one and take it back and get another.
–    Are you a monk, or?
–    A monk?
–    I've never seen such a – You don't have anything.
–    I just don't feel the need to have much.
     We can go out if you want.
–    No, it's fine.


–    I'm going to buy you a lamp or something.
–    It's light enough.
–    It's like a cell.
     Did you buy those curtains?
–    They were just here when I moved in.
–    You're not a big decorator.
–    Not – Not really.
–    But you work – I mean, you sell people –
–    Stuff to do up their houses, yeah.
–    But you've never been tempted.
–    No. I don't really – It's fine. Sorry.
–    It's just really lonely. Makes me sad.


–    Oh, I got you these.
     You know.
–    What for?
–    Well, it's just.
     Been a few months now, hasn't it.

–  You've been counting?
–  Not – Counting, but. I've got a fair idea. Few months.


–  They alright?
–  They're lovely.

–  I like it. This. Us.

–  Me too.

**6**

—   This ends *here*, Evil Man! I've foiled your plots to blow
up the world, to turn everyone in the world into your
slaves, and your plot to give everyone an arse for a
face. Now I've cornered you in this burning building
it's *over*. I'm sick of it.

—   Fine. Do your worst Amazing.

—   Oh right, you're sorry now, are you?

—   You just don't understand. You have no idea.

—   Oh, I've got plenty of ideas. Ideas of how to punch you
in the face.

—   I wasn't always evil you know. I used to have a different
life, before all of this, before all of these plots.

—   Pull the other one.

—   Before I was known as Evil Man, my name was Good
Man. And I was the most good person in the world.

—   I don't believe it.

—   It's true. Check my driver's licence. I was Good Man.

And I was married to a beautiful princess, and we had three small puppies who were always licking my face.

— What happened?

— One night I was rescuing some orphans from a factory, and I accidentally fell into a barrel of Evil Juice. I didn't know it, but the Evil Juice was made of acid and fire and Hitler's poop. When I swam out of the Evil Juice I realised that my whole face had changed and become evil. And so had my brain. I went home to my Princess wife, but she just slammed the door in my face because I ate our three puppies, because I was evil.

— Well. That is a sad story. But it still doesn't excuse what you've done to this planet. Sometimes bad things happen. But you can't take those bad things out on other people.

— I know that, don't you think I know that? I've made mistakes Amazing –

— We should probably head outside, the fire's spread to the roof now.

— Of course I've made mistakes. But it's so hard to be good, when the whole world expects you to be Evil.

— Can't you give me another chance Amazing? As we stand here, man to man, in this burning house?

Amazing?

Amazing?

Are you listening?

**7**

–   Pregnant.
–   Yes.
–   Pregnant with a –
–   With a baby.
–   With a –
–   With a *person*, yes.



–   You already –
–   I went and I had the *scan*, and –
–   So you've known –
–   I didn't tell you because I didn't want to have the
     conversation where you say 'Let's think about this'
     which actually means 'Let's think about abortion'.
–   I wouldn't –
–   Because we're not. I'm keeping – She's staying.
     And you can be involved,

Or not.
You can stay or go but you can't –
It's happening.
This is a, a, *thing* –
That's happening.

–   She's a she already.
–   It's a girl.
–   They can tell this soon?
–   No, they didn't – I just know.
–   You know it's a girl?
–   Yes.
–   You're guessing.
–   I just know.


–   You're not saying anything . . .
–   Because I'm – I'm just a little bit, uh, *surprised* –
–   Shell-shocked.
–   I would have said surprised –
–   Because you're –
–   Because I'm not very articulate, I know –
–   I wasn't – saying that –
–   It's alright.
–   Okay.


–   Sorry.

–   I'm sorry I didn't tell you. Before.


–   Do you hate me?


–   What?
–   Do you hate me now?
–   Of course not.

–    No?
–    No. Course not. I'm just, you know –


–    I mean. Do you *want* me to stay?
–    Do I *want* you to stay.
–    You said I could stay or go, do you *want* me to stay?
–    Of course I do.


–    Okay.

–    Okay?
–    Just. Of course. Yes.
     Three of us.


–    I was really hoping you'd say that.

## 8

Ball.

Ball . . .

Ball.

Uh –
Carpet.

Car-pitt.

Ball.

Chair.

You sit in chairs.

See?

Chair.


Tree.

Tree.

Trees grow out of the ground –
And, uh –
Through something called photo-syn-the-sis –
They turn sun – That's the sun –
Into food. Tree food.
Or – Wait –
Or they turn carbon diox-ide –
Into oxygen.
Which we breathe.
And that makes us alive.
It's one of those two, I don't, uh . . .


Ball.

Trousers.

Men wear trousers – And –
Well.
People wear trousers.
Sometimes girls wear trousers too –
You can wear trousers when you grow up, if you want –
Now. You can wear them now. Wear what you want.


Shoes.

Daddy is wearing shoes.

Daddy.

Da-dee.

Daddy wears shoes.

**9**

–   Dog.
–   Dog, yes.


–   Dog.
–   Dog.


–   Dog.
–   Yes. Okay.
–   Dog.
–   We don't have a dog, sweetheart.

–   No.

–   Okay.

–   No.
–   No?
–   No.
–   Okay.

–    No.
–    No wh –
–    Dog.
–    Dog again.
–    No.
–    Daddy?


–    Dad?

–    Daddy?
–    Dog.
–    Daddy.
–    Dog.

–    Daddy?
–    No.
–    Okay.

**10**

—  What if no one likes me?
—  Well – They'll like you. People will like you.
—  What if they don't?
—  There's a lot of kids here. I'm sure someone will like you.
    . . .
    They'll like you, of course they'll like you.
—  What if the teachers don't like me.
—  The teachers have to like you, it's their job. They have
       to like everybody.
—  What if the teacher thinks I'm not doing any work and
       I get told off.
—  Well do your work, then.
—  What if the teacher thinks I'm not doing it but I am.
—  Well they won't think that then.
—  What if they do and I get told off and expelled.
—  I don't –
—  What if that happens?
—  I don't think that'll happen.

- It might.
- I doubt it. Just don't – You'll have fun. It's good.
    School's good.

- Can you come in with me?
- No.
- Why?
- Because. School's for children. I've done school.
    I finished.
- Did you ever get told off at school?
- N – Well – Sometimes.
- Why?
- Because I wasn't working hard enough –
- Why not?
- Because I was stupid.
- Why?
- I don't know why. I just was.
- But not now.
- Sometimes now too.
- You're stupid now?
- Sometimes. Everyone is sometimes.

- Are you crying?
- No.
- Why are you crying?
- I'm not.
- You are.
- My eyes are just watering.
- They're not.
- It's windy, and – It's the wind.
- What are you crying about?
- Nothing. I'm not.


- I'm not.


- Now you better – You don't wanna be late.

—    Will you pick me up?
—    Mum'll pick you up.
—    What time?
—    Just after three.
—    Three fifteen.
—    Yes.
—    What if she's late?
—    She won't be.
—    What if she's late and I get kidnapped.
—    I don't – That's not – Don't talk to strangers.
—    I don't.
—    Then you won't –
—    What if they just pick me up and run away with me?
—    Just – That won't happen.
—    It might.
—    Well – Just don't talk to strangers.

—    Come on, the bell went already.

—    Bye Dad.

—    Bye.

      . . .

      . . .

      . . .

# 11

- And that's the last time I tumble dry my costume.
- Mm-hm.
- Do you realise how hard it is to fight crime, when your costume's so tight your balls are practically inside your anus?

  I don't need to give the Joker any *more* reasons to laugh, you know what I'm saying?
- Hm.
- So what's going on with you?
- Not much −
- Did I tell you the fucking batmobile broke down *again*?
- No −
- Right in the middle of a high-speed chase, it just − frrt − stops.
- Do you want another beer?
- No I'm fine − I had to continue the chase in the bat jet.
- Okay.
- But my insurance is starting to go through the roof, I've had it towed three times this month alone. Maybe I should just start using the bat bike more often. But obviously it's not as heavily armoured as the car so it's like hello, anyone order a sitting duck? You know?

What's wrong with you?
- I'm just bored.
- Of what?
- Of listening to you.
- . . . What?
- Do you realise why Superman never wants to hang out
   with you any more?
- He sometimes –
- It's because he's sick – we're *all* sick of listening to you
   moan about how hard it is to be Batman.
- We're talking here –
- No, *you're* talking, I'm struggling to care –
- Hey, come on –
- You were lucky anyone was willing to spend time with
   you in the first place, and now you've totally
   outstayed your welcome.
- What's that supposed to mean?
- It means you forced your way into our circle.
- Your circle?
- No one wanted you around, you're not a superhero.
- Oh, I'm not a superhero.
- No.
- Okay.
- You're not.
- Sure, I'm not a superhero.
- No.
- You think I like to wear all this leather for fun?
- Maybe. I don't know.
- I'm out there *every* night, keeping the peace.
- Alright –
- Dealing with the scum of the streets –
- With what?
- What?
- What are you using to combat all this crime?
- I'm –
- What powers do you have?
- Oh come on –
- What powers do you have?

- I'm sick of justifying myself to you fascists.
- I'm saying. Superheroes like hanging out with
  superheroes. We share common ground.
- I share common ground.
- You're just a billionaire with a leather fetish.
- Hey take that back!
- We only put up with you because you buy all the drinks.
- Fuck you Amazing! I know you're just jealous.
- Course I am.
- I'm sorry if I want to talk about real crime fighting,
  instead of listening to you whine about your marriage.
- Okay –
- 'My wife hates me.' 'We never talk any more.'
- Shut up –
- 'Everything's different now.'
- What would you know, bachelor?
- Whatever – I don't need to sit here and listen to this
  I've got work to do –
- Counting your millions of dollars?
- No, I have to go and pick up the dry cleaning for the
  Justice League, which I am a part of, because I'm a
  fucking *superhero*!

**12**

- So your mum and I –
- Put that down sweetheart –
- We –
- Emily –
- What?
- You have to listen, this is important.
- I can't get –
- Just put it down.

- So me and your mum –
- Your dad and I are going to separate.

- What's that?
- . . .
- That means we're not going to live together any more.

- What?
- No – Sweetheart –
- You're moving away?

-   No – Not away –
-   Your dad's going to rent the house next door, and –
-   Why?
-   Because – It's a very complicated –
-   You hate each other.
-   No! Nononono –
-   We don't *hate* each other.
-   We just . . . *Think* that – We don't get along as well as
       we used to, and –
-   It's making us sad, and we don't want to make *you* sad –
-   You're making me sad right now.
-   It'd make you more sad if we didn't do this.
-   Why?
-   Because . . .
-   Because we'd be arguing all the time, and –
-   Why?
-   Because we feel angry with each other a lot –
-   Why?
-   Because –
-   What did you do?
-   No one *did* anything –
      It's just –
      Grown-ups sometimes have to do this.
-   Why?
-   Just . . . Because.


-   You'll still see your dad every day.
-   No I won't.
-   Course you will. Won't she?
-   Yeah. Course. Of course.
-   He's just living next door.
-   No he's not.
-   Well he will be.


-   Are you getting divorced?
-   You know what divorced means?

-   We're not – It's sort of – Yes.
-   We are?
-   (I'm just trying to explain it . . . )
-   And you don't love each other.
-   No, we – We still do.
-   Course.
-   You don't.
-   Emily –
-   I don't think you do.
-   Well. We do.
-   Then why can't you live in this house?
-   Because . . . Life is strange sometimes.


-   Why?
-   Stop asking why all the time please sweetheart.
-   But I don't understand.
-   Well. You will. Won't she?
    Hm?
-   Yeah.
    . . .
    Yes.

# 13

–   This is your room.


–   It's big. It's quite a big room, so –
–   Is this my duvet?
–   Yeah, that's – It's Spider-Man.
–   Yeah.
–   You like Spider-Man.
–   He's okay.
–   He's okay. Well.
–   I have a duvet.
–   Yes.
–   In Mum's house.
–   Well now you've got two.


–   Okay.
–   Okay?
–   Okay.


–   How come I don't have a grandma or grandad?
–   What?
–   How come?
–   I –
–   They're dead.

–    Well – Most of them.
–    Not all?
–    My dad is still –
–    He's not dead?
–    No, but –
–    Can we meet him?
–    I don't think so.
–    Why?
–    Because we had an argument.
–    About what?
–    Lots of things. He drinks too much.
–    Too much alcohol.
–    Yes.
–    And that's why.
–    Lots of reasons.
–    Isn't it better to make up with people.
–    Yes. Course.
–    So why don't you.
–    Because it's complicated.
–    Why?
–    Because – Come on. Emily.


–    I thought we could have a special tea.


–    Emily?
–    Like what?
–    Like a Chinese takeaway.
–    I don't know what that is.
–    It's food from China.
–    How does it get here?
–    Well they make it here, and then –
–    Then how is it Chinese?
–    Because Chinese people – Uh – It – It just is.


–    It's cold in this house.

—    Well . . . why don't we wrap you up in your duvet?

—    That better?
—    (*Nods.*)
—    In your duvet suit.
—    Like a cape.
—    Like a cape.

## 14

–   Do you remember how you felt before it happened?
–   (*Shakes head.*)
–   No?
–   Did you feel sick?
–   (*Shrugs.*)
–   Did you get dizzy?
–   (*Shrugs.*)
–   You don't remember anything?
–   (*Shakes head.*)
–   All we want to do is work out what happened so that it
        doesn't happen again.
–   Did you see any flashing lights?
–   (*Shrugs.*)
–   Flashing lights?
–   Epilepsy.
–   She didn't have a fit –
–   Well I'm just trying –
–   Don't get worked up –

-     I'm not, but you –
-     Stop fighting.

-     Sorry.
-     Sorry.
-     I won't do it again.
-     Do what?
-     I won't fall over again.

**15**

- You're younger than most dads.
- Yes.
- Why?
- Just because.
- You had me younger.
- Yes.
- By having sex.
- Well. Yes. We don't need to –
- So that's why you're younger.
- Yes.
- But you're still bald.
- Well, not –
- No superheroes are bald.
- No?
- No.
- I bet some are –
- No. Lex Luthor is. But he's a bad –
- He's a baddie, yes.
- Dr Charles Xavier is bald.
- Who's he?

- He's the dad of the X-Men.
- Well there you are.
- But he doesn't do much. He's in a wheelchair because he's a cripple.
- Don't say cripple sweetheart.
- Well he is.
- You don't say 'cripple'.
  Some words hurt people's feelings.
  Like cripple.
  And bald.
- Was I an accident?
- What?
- Daniel at school said I was an accident.
- Well he should mind his own fucking business.
- Don't swear Dad.
- Sorry.
- So I am?
- No, that's not –
- So you did want me?
- We want you *now* –
- But not before.
- No, that's not –
- You didn't want me before?
- If you let me speak for five seconds I'll tell you.
  Alright?
  You talk too much.
- Mum says I'm curious.
- Well I say you talk too much.
- Mum says I have to talk to you to make us have a better relationship.

- Dad?
- I'm thinking. Hang on.

- Look, sometimes –
  Sometimes things you –
  Not everything that's *meant* to happen is good.
  And sometimes –

Sometimes things that happen by accident –
Those things can be wonderful.

Alright?

Okay.

**16**

– Okay –
  Thanks for –
– Not at all –
– I just thought it'd be good to, to *touch base*.
– Yes.


– So, I mean –
  We *absolutely* appreciate you coming back –
  Of course we do.
  Of course.
  It's just –
  Well.
  We worry –
  We're somewhat, ah, *concerned* – That you might not be
    *ready* to come back to work for us.


– Okay.
– I know, of course, that you've had a tough time recently –
  You know we all know that.
  And maybe, sometimes, just, you know, getting back on
    the old horse is the way forward.
  But we feel there's certain –

Ah –
We're concerned that you're maybe not quite prepared
    ah, *emotionally*.
Yes.


– So . . . ?
– So, I, *we*, think,
    *maybe*
    you should go home.

– Now?
– Well not this *second* –
    But,
    today.


– So I'm fired?
– No! Nonononono –
    No one's firing anyone here Mark.
– Captain Amazing.

– I'm sorry?
– Captain Amazing.


– Yes. Well. No one's firing anyone here . . .
– . . .
– . . .
– Captain –
– Captain Amazing. Yes. We just feel that maybe,
    you take –
    some *time*,
    Until you feel that you can come to work, perhaps . . .
        *not* wearing the cape.


– You don't like my cape?

–    Oh!
     It's not that we don't like it Mar – Captain.
     It's just,
     Well.
     We do have uniform regulations here.
–    I'm still wearing the uniform.
–    Yes.
–    Just got the cape on –
–    Over the top, yes.
–    Because I need to wear my cape.
–    But at work . . . ?
–    At work, not at work, everywhere.
–    I see.
–    I'm a superhero.
–    . . .
–    The cape sort of goes with that.
–    You . . . need it to fly?
–    I don't need it to fly, it's just a cape – Capes don't make
        people fly –
–    Oh, no –
–    I don't need it to fly Mike, I can fly without the cape.
     It's just a, a, a, *visual* thing. It lets people know.


–    That you're a superhero –
–    That I'm a superhero, yes.
     I don't need a cape to *fly*, Mike.
–    No, sorry.
–    You fucking idiot.
–    I'm sorry Captain.
–    You don't have a clue do you?
–    Now come on, this is hard for everyone.
–    Doesn't seem too hard for you.
–    Now –
–    It *should* be. It *should* be hard.
–    It is.

\-    Do you know how many managers would like to have a
           superhero on their payroll?
       A lot. A lot. And I think it's,
       *Extremely* short-sighted of you to let one slip through
           your fingers.
       The potential benefits here that you're not – You know.
\-    Captain –
\-    And who the fuck are you to ask me about my emotional
           state?
\-    I, I –
\-    I could burn this place to the ground with my heat
           vision, do you really think it's a good idea to piss me
           off?
\-    Okay, let's –
\-    You should be doing *everything* in your power to keep me
           happy,
       But you're too *stupid* to even realise what you've got in
           front of you.
       You're an *ant*.
       You're *nothing.*
       I'm a *god*. I'm fucking *Hercules.*
       You'd have to be *insane* to let me just walk out your
           door.

       Don't you think?

# 17

- Alright. You're going to sleep.
- I bet I won't.
- You will.
- I won't.
- You want the door open?
- Will you read me a story?
- No, it's late.
- Please?
- You said you'd go straight to sleep if I let you stay up.
- Yeah –
- And I did. So. That's your side of the bargain.
- But –
- That's your side. It's late. What time is it?
- It's not that late.
- It's late.


- I'm not reading anything long.
- No.
- Get your shortest –

—    Make up a story.
—    That's not reading, is it?
—    It's easier.
—    No it's not.
—    But –
—    Emily –
—    Please.


—    About what? Who's it about, you?
—    No.
—    Who's it about?
—    I don't know. You.
—    Me? You don't want to hear a story about me.
—    I do.
—    I don't have any stories that are –
—    You have to make one up.


—    About what?
—    Use your imagination!


—    Are you a superhero?
—    What?
—    Do you have powers? That can be the story.
—    Fine. Yes.
—    You've got powers.
—    Yes.
—    Like what?
—    Just, you know. All of them.
—    You have to be specific.
—    That's a good word. How long have you been saying
          specific?
—    It's just a word.
—    I'm impressed.
—    You're impressed by anything. What are your powers?
—    I don't know . . . I can fly. I guess.

–   You can fly.
–   And fire . . . things from my eyes . . .
–   Lasers.
–   Fine. Lasers.
–   And what else?
–   . . . See through walls . . . and . . .
–   Dad you're falling asleep.
–   I'm not . . .
–   Dad.
–   I'm resting my eyes. I'm listening.
–   What's your name?
–   What?
–   Your name as a superhero.
–   Just, you know . . . Captain . . .

–   Captain What?
–   Amazing. Mr Amaz – Captain Amazing.


–   That's the worst name Dad.
–   It's fine . . .
–   That's the worst superhero name ever made.
    What do you do as Captain Amazing?
–   Fight . . . baddies and things. Save people.
    . . . make people go to bed when they're supposed to
    go to bed . . .
    . . .
    . . .
–   Dad?


–   Are you asleep?


–   Dad?


–   Good night.

–   . . .
–   . . .

## 18

–   Hey-

–   Hey. Superman –
–   . . .
–   Superman –
–   Oh! Captain Amazing, Hi!
–   I was trying to – But –
–   Yeah, yeah. The wind, you know.
–   I can't hear a fucking thing.
–   How've you been?
–   Wha?
–   *How've you been?*
–   Oh, fine, fine.
–   I heard you and Mrs Amazing-?
–   Yeah, we've separated.

– Sorry to hear that.
– What?
– *I said I'm sorry to hear that.*
– It's okay. It was probably time.

– How's your kid?
– Oh, yeah, she uh –
– She's at school now?
– Yeah, just started.
– How's she – Ah!

– You alright?
– Fucking birds.
– Tell me about it.

– Well. I'd better go.
– Alright.
– I'd stay and chat, but –
– I know you're busy. Nice to see you.
– You too man. I'll see you around.

**19**

–   Emily –
–   Emily can you put that –
–   Emily, listen.

–   We –
–   Every time we sit like this you tell me something bad.
–   Well, that's –
–   Every time!

–   Look –
–   What?
–   Emily.

–   The Doctor says –
–   Can I go back to school?
–   Well, that's what we're – Can you help me out here?
–   Sweetheart –

–   The Doctor says it's going to take a bit longer.
    And that's why –
    You know.


–   So he says we have to work hard to make you, to get
        better.
–   Work hard?
–   Yes.
–   You have to be strong.
–   I'm not strong.
–   Course you are.
–   I can't even open the jam.
–   Not that kind of – Like a different strong.
–   Headstrong.
–   Headstrong.
–   Strong in the head?
–   Yes.
–   Like headbutting things.
–   No –
–   Just brave. It just means brave.
–   Why do I have to be brave?
–   Because you're poorly.
–   I get poorly all the time.

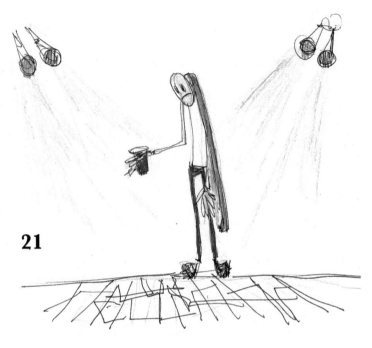

**21**

- I'm a superhero.

- I'm a *superhero*. Can you hear me?
- Can you hear me?
- Hey –
- Can you please leave me alone?
- We're just having a conversation –
- No, you're just shouting at me.
- Sorry.
- Drunk.
- I'm just telling you –
- I don't care what you're dressed as.
- I'm not *dressed* as anything, I'm Captain Amazing.
- Okay. Fine. Go away.
- I'm the real thing –
- Leave her alone, mate.

-    I'm just having a conver*sation*, why's everyone –
-    Go *away* –
-    You don't have to be such a bitch about it –
-    Piss off –
-    Alright mate, time to leave.
-    We're *talking* here –
-    Outside.

## 20

—   I'm always asleep.
—   That's okay.
—   It's boring.
—   It's not boring if you're asleep, is it?
—   Yes.
—   How can it be if you're sleeping?

—   It's boring being tired all the time.

—   Are you tired now?
—   (*Nods.*)


—   Am I more like you or more like Mum?
—   You're, ah, more like your Mum. You're better than me.
—   I'm not like you?
—   Well, okay, you've got – You've got bits of both of us.
       But you got most of your good bits from Mum.
—   Mum says you don't like yourself very much.
—   Well Mum – tells you things I wish she wouldn't.
—   Why don't you?
—   I do – I mean – I'm alright. Don't worry about me.
—   Sometimes I do.

–    Worry?
–    (*Nods.*)
–    About what?
–    That you're sad. You're sad all the time.

–    Well don't.
    Just –
    Concentrate on yourself.


–    Dad?
–    What?
–    I'm sorry I'm so boring.
–    You're not boring, stop saying that.
–    All I do is sleep and be sick.
–    That's fine.
    That's enough.


–    Do you know what's going to happen next?


–    No.


–    I don't.
–    But no one knows sweetheart.
    Not even your doctor.
    No one knows anything either way.

    I know I'm your dad and that means I should know
       everything,
    But,
    I just don't.
    I don't know.
    . . .
    I used to think my dad knew everything.
    I used to think he was indestructible.

Built from bricks and stone.
And it's hard – when you find out that's not true,
But it happens to everyone.
It's just happened to you a bit sooner than most.
. . .
But none of that means I won't be here with you.
Whatever happens,
Me and your mum will be right with you.
You don't have to be scared about anything,
Because we'll be here.
But if you're asking what's going to happen tomorrow,
Or,
Or, the day after that –
. . .
I just don't know.
But I do know I'll be here.

–   I don't really think you're a superhero Dad.
–   I know.
–   It was just a game.
–   Yeah.
–   And you don't have to play it any more.

**21**

- I'm a *superhero*.
- You like harassing girls?
- I was just *talking* to her. If she doesn't want to talk to
    me –
- She doesn't.
- Well if you let me go back in then I won't –
- You're not going back in.
- Hey, I'm a *superhero* –
- No one gives a shit who you think you are –
- I don't *think* anything. I *am*. I *am*.
- You're going home.
- Hey –
- Go home –
- I'm a superhero, you don't talk to superheroes that way –
- Walk away.
- Hey. Heyheyhey –
- Walk away or we'll fall out, alright?
- Come on.

Let's not get – UGH –
–    What did I say? What did I say to you?
–    You don't want to do that again. I don't want to have
        to hurt y-UGH –
–    What did I *tell* you?
–    I don't want to – UGH –
–    You don't w – UGH –
    ********
    *******
    ******
    *****
    ****
    ***
    **
    *


–    . . .
    . . .
    . . .
    . . .
    . . .




–    Yes.
    Yes.
    Yes.


–    Are you
        Are you
            Are you
–    Are you listening to me?
–    Of course.


    What?

–     Of course.
    . . .
–     I think I need to spend some time.
    Away.
    . . .
    I need to not be here for a while.
    In this house.
    Can you understand that?
    Are you listening to me?
    Can you understand why I need to do that?

–     Of course.
    Of course I do.

–     Not for ever.
–     No.
–     But just –
–     It's fine.
–     And you'll be alright?
–     Yes.
–     . . .
–     . . .
–     I'll let you know.
    Wherever I end up, and you can call me.
    If anything –
    You can just call me.
    . . .
    Promise you'll do that.
–     Captain Amazing!
–     Promise you'll call me if you need to –
–     Captain Amazing we need your help!
–     Are you listening to me?
–     Yes. Course. Of course I will –
–     Captain Amazing we need you! There's an emergency!
–     *Mark.*
–     . . .
–     I'm leaving now, alright?
–     Okay.

Have a –
Good trip.
. . .
. . .

. . .


–    Captain Amazing!
–    What?
–    There's an emergency!
–    The old mill's on fire! There's people trapped inside!
–    I'm, uh –
    What's this now?
–    I drew this.
–    Captain Amazing! Help!
–    I'm coming – I – This is a good drawing –

    The train's headed straight for the cliff!

–    Hang on –

    I like Spider-Man best.

    Men can be nurses as well.

    I fell asleep.

    I was sick on your coat.

–    That's alright –

    I was sick on Mum's bed.

–    Quickly, grab on to me-

    The brakes won't work! She won't stop, Captain!

My tummy's bad.

My baby! My baby's in there!

I fell down again.

–   There's so much smoke . . .

So you wear the cape all day?

–   I can wear what I want –

It's a cape?

It's kind of dirty.

You can't sleep here, sir.

You should consider some sort of spandex.

How long?

How long now?

And for saving the lives of hundreds of our town's
   steelworkers, I award you the key to the city –

–   Thank you-

When can I go back to school?

Speech Captain! Speech!

When can we go home?

Are you okay?

–   It's a great honour to receive this –

This is a very stupid thing to be doing, sir.

And then this lace goes through here . . .

—   Sometimes I feel like there's speech bubbles hanging
        over me —

We'll talk to the doctor.

—   It's all just a part of my job.

That's a good one.

That's me.

And that's Mum.

I drew your head too big.

And too bald.

Sir —

The other girls think I'm weird.

Sir, put that down —

Mark —

Mark —

—   I couldn't afford a big — It's still a diamond. It's a proper
        ring.

Stop that.

Don't touch that.

That's dirty, sweetheart −

Sir!

What did I just say?

Dog

Hat

Shoes

You can't just put on a cape and go around hitting people −

Okay

It'll grow back. They said it'll grow back.

Okay

Get *out* −

−    I'm just starting to feel like everything's overlapping a bit −

Can I try coffee?

Can I try beer?

Can I try wine?

−    I don't −

Can we get a dog?

I don't like cats.

Fuck you.

Captain Amazing, he's getting away!

–    What?

Stop it.

Stop.

That's *enough*.

He's getting *away*!

Get *out* –

Dad –

–    Please –

Dad –

I'll be gone anyway –

Stop that.

I could spin right round the world backwards –

I know –

Fast enough to put time back to dinosaurs –

I know –

I *know* –

Interfering with time is against the superhero code.

–   Fuck you. *Fuck you* –

Sir –

Go home.

You can't be here –

Go *home*.

Even without you writing the stories –

–   This is enough.

He'll still be flying around.

–   This is enough now-

He'll still be having adventures –

–   Please . . .

It's a *cape*.

It's a *CAPE*.

. . .


. . .


. . .


If you give me some idea of the kind of service you'd
   like –

. . .

. . .

Your ice cream is melting.

I know this is a very difficult process.

—    Do you?

Your ice cream is melting.

. . .

. . .

Don't be sad about me

. . .

. . .

. . .

Superheroes . . .

. . .

all need a reason to put on the cape.

. . .

. . .

. . .

—    . . .

. . . *flying* . . .
. . .
is a lot harder than it looks.

Some idiot once said all you needed was a happy
    thought but that's not enough.
It's a lot more work than that.
A lot harder.
It's a,
. . .
It's a very –
*internal* thing,
flight.

You've got to spend a lot of time in your head.
Get used to *living* in here.


Find yourself a nice, wide open space.
A field, or a, a,
. . .
A car park.
Don't worry about the cape for now, that's all just icing.
Stretch off, warm up.
That's important.
Pick a take-off spot.
Don't look straight up in the air, focus just ahead of you,
    relax –
and concentrate on lifting off.

Clear your mind –
Take a breath –
Think *positive*.
And just let go of everything that's tying you to the
    ground.

Even a centimetre at first,
That's an achievement.
Soon you'll be hovering just above the blades of grass.

Practice.

Then try a bit higher.

A bit higher.

Soon you'll be cutting through the air with ease.

It's a long process,
It'll take practice,
But it's worth it.
Flying over the pyramids at night –

Weaving through the rainforests –
The magic of it never fades.
It never gets old.

Every night I take off –
Pushing myself away from the ground,
My house,
My street,
My town,
This country.
Breaking through clouds as I go,
Watching the stars get closer.

I like to glide across the night sky,
Look down at the lights that string the globe,
The glow of the moon in the black sheets of the oceans,

Feel the world and everything in it turning beneath me.

And every night I have the same thought –

I don't know what I'd do without this.

*He smiles.*

*Black.*

# DRAMA ONLINE

# A new way to study drama

From curriculum classics
to contemporary writing
Accompanied by
theory and practice

## Discover. Read.
## Study. Perform.

Find out more:
www.dramaonlinelibrary.com

BLOOMSBURY

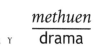
*methuen*
**drama**

THE ARDEN
SHAKESPEARE

ff FABER
DIGITAL

## Bloomsbury Methuen Drama Modern Plays
*include work by*

Bola Agbaje
Edward Albee
Davey Anderson
Jean Anouilh
John Arden
Peter Barnes
Sebastian Barry
Alistair Beaton
Brendan Behan
Edward Bond
William Boyd
Bertolt Brecht
Howard Brenton
Amelia Bullmore
Anthony Burgess
Leo Butler
Jim Cartwright
Lolita Chakrabarti
Caryl Churchill
Lucinda Coxon
Curious Directive
Nick Darke
Shelagh Delaney
Ishy Din
Claire Dowie
David Edgar
David Eldridge
Dario Fo
Michael Frayn
John Godber
Paul Godfrey
James Graham
David Greig
John Guare
Mark Haddon
Peter Handke
David Harrower
Jonathan Harvey
Iain Heggie

Robert Holman
Caroline Horton
Terry Johnson
Sarah Kane
Barrie Keeffe
Doug Lucie
Anders Lustgarten
David Mamet
Patrick Marber
Martin McDonagh
Arthur Miller
D. C. Moore
Tom Murphy
Phyllis Nagy
Anthony Neilson
Peter Nichols
Joe Orton
Joe Penhall
Luigi Pirandello
Stephen Poliakoff
Lucy Prebble
Peter Quilter
Mark Ravenhill
Philip Ridley
Willy Russell
Jean-Paul Sartre
Sam Shepard
Martin Sherman
Wole Soyinka
Simon Stephens
Peter Straughan
Kate Tempest
Theatre Workshop
Judy Upton
Timberlake Wertenbaker
Roy Williams
Snoo Wilson
Frances Ya-Chu Cowhig
Benjamin Zephaniah

For a complete listing of Bloomsbury
Methuen Drama titles, visit:

**www.bloomsbury.com/drama**

Follow us on Twitter and keep up to date
with our news and publications

**@MethuenDrama**

Lightning Source UK Ltd.
Milton Keynes UK
UKHW050501140120
356912UK00007B/105/P